# The Belfast and Moosehead Lake Railroad

Joey Kelley

Copyright © 2017 by Joey Kelley

All rights reserved. No part of this book may be reproduced or transmitted in any form or by any means without written permission of the author.

ISBN 978-1-943424-18-4
Library of Congress Control Number: 2017935265

Front Cover Top Photo – Locomotives #50 and #53 are headed east over Knox Station Road on September 24, 2014. The author is making his first trip as a qualified conductor and can be seen wearing a reflective vest in locomotive #50. The train is bound for City Point after completing Common Ground Fair operations for the year. Photo by Shawn Duren.

Front Cover Bottom Photo -- Locomotive #1149 has just departed Unity Station headed for Burnham Junction. Taken on August 13, 2006, #1149 has only a few months before being found in need of major repairs. Photo by the author.

Rear Cover Background Photo – Locomotive #53 has stopped at Unity's Depot Street on October 15, 1989. Photo by W. A. Gleason, author's collection.


North Country Press
Unity, Maine

To all the railroaders of the Belfast and Moosehead Lake Railroad, paid and volunteer, past and present, this book would not have been possible without you.

# Acknowledgments

Ideally, I would list here everyone who has done anything to keep the Belfast and Moosehead Lake's 150-year history alive. Unfortunately, I need to have some space to actually write about the railroad! Several individuals are directly responsible for my involvement with and love of the Belfast and Moosehead Lake Railroad. A chance meeting with "Mack" Page in 2003 resulted in becoming involved with his private museum, the City Point Central, home of many Belfast and Moosehead Lake artifacts. Former Operations Manager, Paul Hallett, kept me involved as much as my work schedule would allow. Meanwhile, Bruce C. Cooper's history of the Belfast and Moosehead Lake website has kept my historical interest burning. I must thank my former boss, Bob Lamontagne, who ran the Belfast and Moosehead Lake Railroad Preservation Society, for everything he did to keep the wheels turning. Megan Pinette of the Belfast Historical Society dug through the archives to help and provided a lot of background information and photographs. Kevin Johnson at the Penobscot Marine Museum spent a lot of time putting together photos from their collection. All of my fellow volunteers with the Brooks Preservation Society that have worked so diligently since 2008 to preserve, restore and operate the railroad deserve many thanks. The largest single contributor to this book is Mr. Joey J. Feero, executive director of the Brooks Preservation Society. In addition to getting the idea of a book in my head, his generous contribution of photographs has made many images in this book possible. He has of course been instrumental in keeping the Belfast and Moosehead Lake Railroad rolling since 2008. Finally, I must thank my parents, Joe and Pat Kelley, who have encouraged, directly and indirectly, my interests in both history and railroads from a young age.

–Joey Kelley, Brewer, Maine, February 2017

# Introduction

In 1867 a railroad was chartered to run from Belfast, Maine, to Moosehead Lake, approximately 100 miles away. Before it could be completed, the line fell under the control of the Maine Central Railroad and its terminus was changed, effectively cutting off the plan to build to Moosehead Lake. In 1926, the Belfast and Moosehead Lake Railroad began independent operation. With 33 miles of railroad all contained within Waldo County, Maine, this short line railroad has survived two world wars, the collapse of Waldo County's commercial poultry industry and gone into the passenger excursion train business to survive. Prior to being sold to private investors in 1991, the Belfast and Moosehead Lake Railroad is believed to have been unique in the United States in that it was an independent company whose shares were owned primarily by the towns the railroad served. One of only two railroads in North America and the only one in the United States to import a steam locomotive from Sweden in the 1990s, the Belfast and Moosehead Lake Railroad was home to the largest operating steam locomotive in the state of Maine for over two decades. The year 2005 was a bad one for the railroad - the Belfast yard was removed and the property turned to other uses. In 2006, a non-profit took over operations, lasting until the end of 2007. In 2009 the Brooks Preservation Society became the operator of the railroad and remains so until the present day. Celebrating its 150th anniversary in 2017, this railroad holds the distinction of being the only railroad in the State of Maine still operating under the name it was originally chartered under.

# The Beginnings

### The pre-railroad era and 1867-1925

It has been said that the history of America is largely the history of its railroads. The 1860s were a period of great change in the United States. The first half of the decade was dominated by the American Civil War and the effect of that war on American society is hard to understate. Even while the war was still being fought, bills were being passed in Congress to establish what became the first transcontinental railroad. The Civil War proved how effective railroads were at moving massive amounts of people, cargo and war materials at a speed and cost that was unmatched. The more heavily industrialized North, with its accompanying miles of railroad track, had a strategic advantage over the South, with fewer rail lines.

Although today it is hard to imagine, with interstate highway travel in automobiles often at speeds exceeding 70 miles per hour, being able to travel at speeds over 30 miles per hour for extended periods was extraordinary in the 1860s. Many people up until their first train ride never went faster than their horse could go. Animal powered transportation was in many areas the only land transportation until the railroad came. Heavy freight and passenger traffic the world over relied on ships, both for travel between continents and within the same country, even the same state. The value of land was tied to its proximity to a body of water.

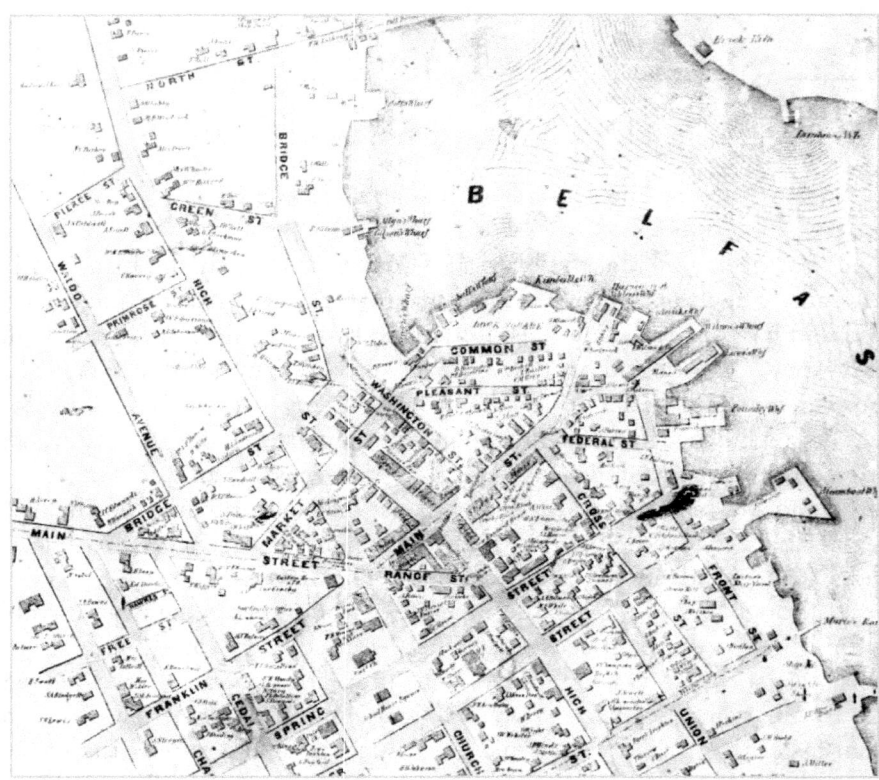

This map, dated 1859, of Belfast showing Puddle Dock and the area that would become known for the Belfast Terminus of the Belfast and Moosehead Lake Railroad. The railroad would be built starting in what is labeled as "Dock Square" just inland from the end of Main Street. (Collection of the Belfast Historical Society and Museum)

The decade between 1860 and 1870 saw the number of miles of railroad track in the United States almost double – from 30,000 to 52,000 miles, all while for the first half of the decade the Civil War was still going on. On February 28, 1867, the charter for the Belfast and Moosehead Lake Railroad was signed by Governor Joshua L. Chamberlain. The State of Maine was approaching its 47th birthday, having gained Statehood in 1820, separating from the Commonwealth of Massachusetts. The Belfast and Moosehead Lake Railroad Company was organized on July 3rd of 1867. The 1867 Belfast and Moosehead Lake Railroad was the third attempt to get a railroad built from Belfast, Maine, and it would be the successful one. The first two attempts, the Belfast and Quebec and the first attempt known as the Belfast and Moosehead Lake Railroad, failed for a lack of money. This time the plan was simple – sell stock, get the money to build the

# Chapter 1

railroad, lay 35 miles of track from Belfast to Newport, Maine, annex the existing Dexter and Newport Railroad then build from Dexter to Greenville, Maine, on the shores of Moosehead Lake.

This 1869 view of Belfast was taken prior to the railroad's completion. (Collection of the Belfast Historical Society and Museum)

Today each year countless people snowmobile and vacation around Moosehead Lake, but in the 1860s the area was rural to say the least. Greenville and the surrounding area was known for logging, but there was no rail connection from the Moosehead Lake region to anywhere. Those familiar with the railroads of the State of Maine today know that the former Canadian Pacific International of Maine division runs right through Greenville on an almost due east-west course from border to border. Although an east-west railroad through Greenville was proposed, and in fact referenced in a pamphlet released by the City of Belfast in 1869, no rail line was actually completed until the Canadian Pacific took over the project and filled in a 100-mile gap in the east-west route.

### Railroad Ties Wanted.

**80,000 RAILROAD TIES.**

To be **Cedar, Hacmetac, Yellow Ash** and **Hemlock**—9 feet long, **6** inch face, and **6** inches thick. Also a quantity of Hemlock or other timber for crib-work. Dimensions will be furnished at the Contractors' office. Parties desiring to furnish the above, or a portion of it, may apply to

**WILLSON, TENNANT & CO.,**

**Contractors B. & M. L. R. R.**

Belfast, Nov. 24, 1869.                                        tf20

Dated November 24, 1869, this advertisement shows that Willson, Tennant & CO. was using locally harvested ties for the construction effort. (Collection of the Belfast Historical Society and Museum)

That was completed in 1889 – 22 years after the Belfast and Moosehead Lake's charter was signed. Construction on the Bangor and Piscataquis started in 1868; it would take them until 1884 to reach Greenville, 17 years after the Belfast and Moosehead Lake's charter was signed. This line would become the Bangor and Aroostook's Greenville Branch when the Bangor and Aroostook incorporated in 1891, taking over the Bangor and Piscataquis. When one looks back on history, a 100-mile railroad connecting Belfast and Greenville seems unlikely, but when the Belfast and Moosehead Lake was chartered, they aimed to do what no one had yet done. If history had taken a few different turns, the Belfast and Moosehead Lake Railroad might have been a significant route to and from Canada.

Belfast, April 27, 1869.

Received of Alfred Walton $2.Five Dollars, Cents, it being the assessment on One Shares of the Capital Stock of the BELFAST & MOOSEHEAD LAKE RAILROAD COMPANY.

W. T. COLBURN, Treasurer.

On April 27, 1869, Mr. Alfred Walton became the proud owner of one share of Capital Stock of the Belfast and Moosehead Lake Railroad Company. (Collection of the Belfast Historical Society and Museum)

# Chapter 1

Belfast was a good port and in the 1860s, when the majority of transportation was just beginning to transition to rail from ship, it was possible that a port with a rail connection could have been an economic boom. Connecting the port of St. John, New Brunswick, with the rest of the Canadian Pacific was in fact the reason the east-west International of Maine division was built – proving that a port available year-round was worth building hundreds of miles of railroad for. Although the promoters were building a railroad, they were most certainly also promoting the rail-sea connection at Belfast. An 1869 pamphlet released by the City of Belfast points out the benefits of Belfast over other possible ports: Belfast is 75 miles closer to Greenville than Portland, and unlike the Penobscot River in Bangor, Belfast does not freeze up for five months out of the year. Figures are also quoted that represent the amount of business the proposed line to Greenville was to carry on an annual basis and although they were "A careful estimate, based upon authentic data" in reality, there is no way to verify or deny the claims of over $200,000 per year of business to be hauled over the railroad. That would be well over $3.5 million dollars today, adjusting for inflation.

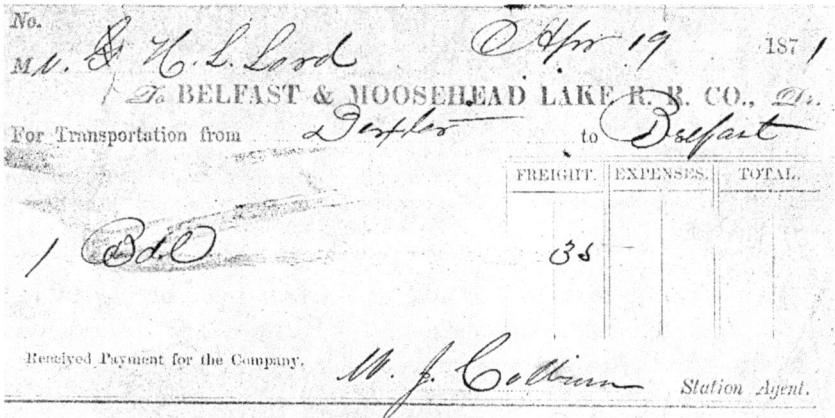

This receipt for freight tendered is dated April 19, 1871. This indicates that before the Maine Central's lease took effect, the railroad was at least running some of its operation using its own name. (Collection of Joey J. Feero)

Rail was cheaper, faster and for the first time, commercial timber and agriculture were possible away from major bodies of water since land transportation was no longer limited to animals. A railroad was an economic boom to an area and if no one else was interested in building it, the citizens of Waldo County decided they would build it themselves. The communities along the right of way bought up the stock, with the city of Belfast being the primary shareholder. Brooks and Unity would buy up the majority of the rest. Then it was a matter of building the railroad: contractors were brought in, steel rails arrived by ship to Belfast and construction started almost literally from the dock where the rail was delivered. Although the railroad was built with cost in mind, it became clear that the railroad would run out of money before they got to Newport.

City Point lies just outside Belfast proper, but still within the modern city limits – facing east, this view shows the 'Beavertail Curve' from the west end – the road known as "High Street" today is on the other side of the tree line on the right. (Postcard dated 1908 – collection of Joey J. Feero)

Belfast's connection to Canada had another stumbling block—the Maine Central Railroad. Chartered in 1862, the Maine Central quickly bought or leased many of the smaller railroads in the State of Maine. Within a few years of the Maine Central's charter, it was well on its way to being the largest railroad in the state. In 1869, two years after the Belfast and Moosehead Lake was chartered, the Maine Central got control of the 30-mile Dexter and Newport. The Dexter and Newport was supposed to be the next phase of the Belfast and Moosehead Lake's thrust Northward. With a change of management, this seemed unlikely. This was the first major blow to the proposed plan to build a railroad from Belfast to Greenville.

# Chapter 1

### Maine Central Time-table.
#### Winter Arrangement.

ON and after Monday, Dec. 3, trains will run as follows: Leave Belfast at 8.15 a.m., City Point 8.20, Waldo 8.34, Brooks 8.50, Knox 9.10, Thorndike 9.20, Unity, 9.30, Leonard's Crossing 9.40, arriving at Burnham at 9.55 a.m.

Leave Belfast at 2.55 p.m., City Point 3.02, Waldo 3.15, Brooks, 3.32, Knox 3.52, Thorndike 4.10, Unity 4.25, Leonard's Crossing 4.35, arriving at Burnham at 4.55 p.m.

Returning—Leave Burnham at 10.20 a. m., Leonard's Crossing 10.32, Unity 10.50, Thorndike 11.03, Knox 11.10, Brooks, 11.38, Waldo 11.56, City Point 12.13, arriving at Belfast at 12.20 p.m.

Leave Burnham at 5.15 p.m., Leonard's Crossing 5.27, Unity, 5.40, Thorndike, 5.54, Knox 6.08, Brooks 6.22, Waldo 6.32, City Point 6.47, arriving at Belfast 6.55 p.m.

Belfast, Dec. 6, 1877.

In this newspaper clipping dated December 6, 1877, the Maine Central lays out the new passenger train schedule for the winter of 1877-1878. The Leonard's Crossing mentioned became known as Winnecook. (Collection of Belfast Historical Society and Museum)

The Maine Central Railroad then entered the picture by proposing to fund the Belfast and Moosehead Lake's completion. Further, they offered a 50-year lease on the railroad. There was a catch however–they moved the terminus of the line to Burnham, Maine, instead of Newport. It was two miles shorter, a bit over 33 miles and since the Maine Central already controlled the Dexter and Newport, there wasn't a whole lot of reason to have another Maine Central controlled railroad in Newport. This was the end of the plan to build from Belfast to Moosehead Lake.

This Westbound passenger train has just left Belfast and is bound for Burnham Jct. This picture is circa 1910, the locomotive appears to be a Maine Central Railroad locomotive. (Collection of Belfast Historical Society and Museum)

In 1870, the Canadian Pacific was just under 20 years away from completing its line through Greenville, and the Bangor and Piscataquis was only a year into construction. Greenville was literally a spot on the map, with no rail significance at the time. The Maine Central may have looked at the investment that would have to be made and decided it was not worth it. They may have looked at the traffic on the Dexter and Newport and decided that it wouldn't justify an expansion. They may also have been tied up in acquiring or building other railroads and did not have the resources or interest to build to Canada. Eventually, the Maine Central would have two lines that would run to the Eastern border of Maine and connect directly with the Canadian Pacific. Whatever the actual motivation was, the Maine Central got its way, the line was built to Burnham and the first scheduled train ran in December 1870. Waldo County finally had its railroad.

# Chapter 1

**Lease**

OF

**BELFAST & MOOSEHEAD LAKE RAILROAD COMPANY**

TO

**MAINE CENTRAL RAILROAD COMPANY.**

APRIL 27, 1871.

This is the front cover of the lease of the Belfast and Moosehead Lake Railroad to the Maine Central Railroad. Signed April 27, 1871, with a May 10, 1871, effective date. (Collection of Joey J. Feero)

The Maine Central signed the 50-year lease on April 27, 1871, with an effective date of May 10, 1871.

Accidents happen – a washout under the track caused this one in September 1909. Engineer Charles F. Shaw was thrown into the harbor. (Collection of Belfast Historical Society and Museum)

What organization ran trains between December 1870 and May 10 of 1871 has been lost to history, but a receipt for freight bound for Belfast dated April 1871 reads "Belfast and Moosehead Lake RR Co." This leads one to think that at least at one point, the railroad was operating under its own name.

# Chapter 1

Maine Central 36 is stopped at the original Brooks Station. The original station was built in 1881, replaced in 1892 with the structure that remains today, after suffering fire damage. (Collection of Joey J. Feero)

Maine Central #194 is discharging passengers at Belfast Station in 1908. The rails literally just stopped in the street. The freight station is the long building on the right-hand side, the freight was delivered on the opposite side of the building, this side was used for loading into road vehicles, either animal drawn or later trucks. (Courtesy of the Lawless Collection, Penobscot Marine Museum)

The rail to sea connection that was so emphasized by the promoters of the railroad was not to be. The railroad was a 'disruptive technology' in modern terms, meaning that one can very easily see the rapid influence of that technology on the culture, economics and people of the time. Intracontinental water transportation vanished as the rail network expanded. International ships no longer called on smaller ports – preferring to call at ports with rail connections like St. John, New Brunswick, Boston, or even New York. Although by no means unique, Belfast's importance as a port shrank as ships got larger and demanded larger and deeper ports.

Taken from along Belfast's Main Street, this undated but early view of the railroad clearly shows the causeway that the railroad built in order to place its terminus near Main Street in Belfast. (Collection of the Belfast Historical Society and Museum)

Combined with the railroad's influence on transportation within the country, the Port of Belfast never really grew to what it could have been – the demand simply wasn't there. The 75 miles that separated Belfast from Portland were now easily traveled by rail – at speeds that were simply not possible with ships. As is the case with many railroads around the country, industries began to stretch along the railroad's track.

# Chapter 1

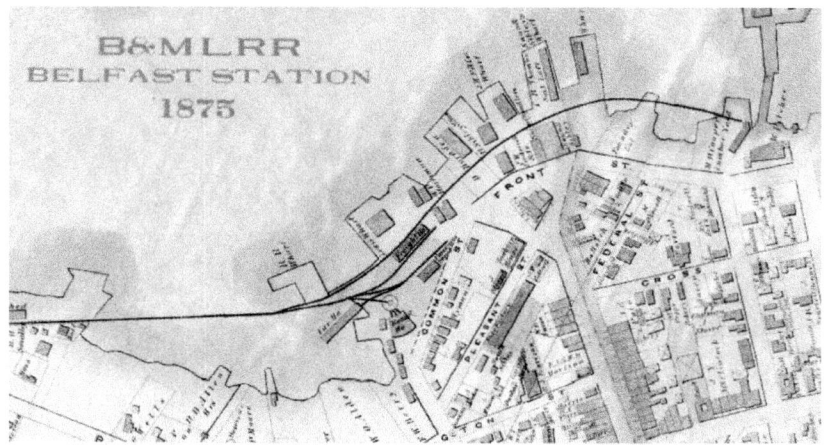

This 1875 map shows the arrangement of tracks along the Belfast waterfront – although it is labeled "B&MLRR" – the line was under lease at this time to the Maine Central. (Collection of the Belfast Historical Society and Museum)

Waldo County's agriculture-based economy provided everything from crops to chickens to milk and eggs to be shipped out on the railroad and manufactured goods from across the continent to be shipped in. Among these were numerous creameries. A creamery is a good industry for a railroad to have as it provides not only loaded cars out, but often ships its raw materials in on the railroad as well. Farmers would milk their cows, the unprocessed milk would be put into cans or other containers, it would be taken to the nearest railroad station (or perhaps directly to a creamery if it were close enough), and the railroad would take the milk to the destined creamery where it would be turned into cream and other dairy products. In the past, the milk you drank in Brooks or Unity, Maine, would often have originated in that town, from cows grazing nearby.

Eastbound Maine Central #198 is stopped at Brooks Station, Brooks, Maine, circa 1918. (Collection of Matthew D. Cosgro, Charles A. Townsend real photo postcard)

World War I was still over a year away from conclusion when this photo was taken. The crowd has gathered to see Waldo County's men off to war. September 19, 1917. (Penobscot Marine Museum Collection)

# Chapter 1

Each year the board of directors of the railroad would meet and the lease payments paid by the Maine Central would be distributed. In general, these payments went out in the form of dividends to the stockholders. Being the primary stockholder, the City of Belfast received the majority of the dividends. By the end of 1925, when all dividends paid were totaled, the City of Belfast had received a total of $834,171.79. On a capital investment of approximately $500,000, the City of Belfast had profited over $300,000 in addition to the obvious and impossible to calculate economic benefits of faster, cheaper and reliable land transportation via the railroad. In addition, the Maine Central Railroad built new stations, laid heavier rail and made other improvements. In effect, the railroad was worth more in 1925 than when it was completed in 1870.

This shot of the 'New' Brooks Station with an eastbound train approaching is dated 1912. Although the freight station is gone, the passenger station still remains. (Scanned real photo postcard, collection of Joey J. Feero)

# The Belfast and Moosehead Lake Railroad

Thorndike Station is shown in this postcard view with a 1910 postmark. (Collection of Joey J. Feero)

An eastbound is approaching Thorndike station in this postcard view, very likely taken on the same day as the previous postcard, considering the same boxcar is behind the station in both views. (Collection of Joey J. Feero)

# Chapter 2

## Independence – 1926-1945

The Belfast and Moosehead Lake Railroad decided to put a float in a parade in 1926 – this shot shows the Belfast Station from an angle not usually photographed. The slogan "Ship and Travel by Rail" was proudly emblazoned on the side of the float. (Courtesy of the Belfast Historical Society and Museum)

Some are under the impression that the Maine Central Railroad owned the Belfast and Moosehead Lake Railroad. Although the Maine Central leased the Belfast and Moosehead Lake, it never owned it outright, although it was not for lack of trying. The Maine Central actually extended its original 50-year lease by another five years but in 1925 announced formally to the Belfast and Moosehead Lake's directors that it would be terminating the lease on December 31, 1925. At the time, the Maine Central claimed it was losing a considerable sum of money each year running the 33-mile line. The directors of the Belfast and Moosehead Lake tried to sell the railroad to the Maine Central, but an agreement could not be reached. Looking back through history, this was a good business decision for the Maine Central. The Belfast and Moosehead Lake Railroad was a feeder line to the Maine Central's main line from Waterville to Bangor. No matter who owned or who ran the Belfast and Moosehead Lake, all traffic would have to come over the Maine Central. Even if the original 35-mile route to Newport had been built, the only connecting railroad would still have been the Maine Central.

# The Belfast and Moosehead Lake Railroad

This view shows the west side of Thorndike station, with Farwell Brothers in the background. This postcard view is circa 1930 and appears courtesy of Matthew D. Cosgro.

By 1925, the railroad was how freight and passengers moved. Travel by ship within the North American continent had all but vanished and inexpensive commercial aviation was still decades away. The automobile and the truck were making themselves felt, but long distance travel was still done primarily by train. Although different in major population centers, in Maine, most roads were little more than dirt tracks, making travel by road difficult and in some cases during the winter, roads would even be closed. By this time sailing ships had largely given way to steam ships and many continued to call on Belfast. As the major shipping routes took advantage of rail transportation, the steam ships coming into Belfast were more likely to contain bulk fuel shipments or be local traffic, such as an island ferry.

## Chapter 2

B&ML 16 appears ready for a westbound passenger run in Belfast. Based upon the lighting direction, this is most likely the afternoon train. (Dated April 1934, Feero Collection)

Today, it would not be uncommon for a railroad to be operated by a contracted railroad firm, but owned by someone else. In the 1920s, however, that arrangement was not common and the Belfast and Moosehead Lake Railroad emerged from its lease on January 1, 1926. The board of directors suddenly found themselves in the position of hiring management and running the railroad. Prior to this, the only real function of the board of directors was an annual meeting. By the end of 1926, the railroad was showing a small profit, despite the claim that the Maine Central had lost money each year it operated the railroad.

B&ML 17 has almost reached its destination, Belfast, with this eastbound train. Today, this same view is dominated by the concrete bridge carrying US Route 1 over the water. (Dated July 15, 1936, Feero Collection)

The expense of leasing the steam locomotives, passenger cars and other equipment needed to run a railroad was considerable and the management bought second-hand steam locomotives from the Bangor and Aroostook Railroad and bought other rolling stock from various railroads including the Boston and Maine. The Belfast and Moosehead Lake would buy equipment that had already seen a good deal of service and run it until the cost to repair it was more than the cost to replace.

Chapter 2

Belfast and Moosehead Lake Railroad #20 is eastbound about 1.5 miles from Belfast, on the 'Whaleback' Curve. Today, this portion of the railroad is now a walking trail. Circa 1935. (Collection of Joey J. Feero)

Wooden passenger cars found a home on the Belfast and Moosehead Lake, even as they were replaced by steel cars on the larger railroads. One, a wooden Boston and Maine Rail Post Office and Baggage car found a new home on the Belfast and Moosehead Lake. Run in regular service for many years, then converted into a tool car for hauling maintenance of way equipment, this particular coach was eventually placed on the ground as a tool shed and carpenter's shop. Used in Belfast yard for over four decades, it was moved to the museum at City Point and still remains, well beyond the average life expectancy of a wooden passenger car.

Belfast and Moosehead Lake Railroad #18 is stopped at Thorndike Station, Thorndike, Maine. Circa 1935. (Collection of Joey J. Feero)

Maine's railroads have traditionally hauled wood and wood products and hauled a lot of them. The Belfast and Moosehead Lake was no exception. For the 29-year period between 1926 and 1955 pulpwood, traditionally softwood used for making paper, was one of the top three commodities hauled by the railroad for 27 of those years. Logged throughout Waldo County, pulpwood would be transported to the railroad and then loaded onto flat cars, after being cut down to a standard length. The logs would then go to one of the paper mills and begin the process of becoming paper.

# Chapter 2

Belfast and Moosehead Lake Railroad #18 drifts downgrade eastbound toward Thorndike station in Thorndike, Maine. Today the area to the left of the photographer is Bryant's Stove Works. Circa 1935. (Collection of Joey J. Feero)

The Belfast and Moosehead Lake rarely bought freight cars. They simply paid the day rate lease for cars from the national freight car pools. The Crash of 1929 and the depression that followed sent many a railroad down an economic path that it would never recover from. Railroads with a traffic base that was based in manufactured goods were the hardest hit. Waldo County's economy was largely agricultural and although traffic dropped by as much as 50% compared to the mid-1920s, the railroad was still vital to the economy of Waldo County.

This circa 1932 view of Brooks, looking east, shows the road that would become Route 7, and the arrangement of the main line and siding that remains to this day. If you look past the poles just left of center, you'll see a building – that is the original Brooks Station, which suffered fire damage and was replaced with the one that remains today. (Courtesy of the Eastern Collection, Penobscot Marine Museum)

Milk continued to be brought to local stations and sent to the creameries on the line for processing.

This canning plant and creamery are still in Brooks, Maine, although you'd be hard pressed to see them through the trees that have grown up since this circa 1932 view. The photographer is standing railroad east from the Route 7 crossing, looking east. (Courtesy of the Eastern Collection, Penobscot Marine Museum)

Chapter 2

After the depression's grip upon the nation subsided, an unfortunate consequence of the rise of the automobile was the decline in passenger rail traffic.

This late 30s, early 40s postcard view of Belfast shows the passenger station and its proximity to the freight tracks. The station and covered platform were unique on the B&ML. (Courtesy of Matthew D. Cosgro)

A Linwood W. Moody article in the October 1940 issue of Railroad Magazine states that of the 14 years of independent operation a total profit of over $100,000 had been made and that only five of those years had shown a deficit. As of Mr. Moody's writing, 28 employees were on the Belfast and Moosehead Lake payroll.

Bangor and Aroostook #60 was sold to the B&ML as #20 in 1940. True to its frugal shortline buying practices, the B&ML bought all its steam locomotives used. (photographer unknown, author's collection)

This easterly-looking view of Belfast shows the circa 1942 arrangement of Belfast Yard. The covered bridge-like structure on the left is a scale for weighing freight cars, the freight station is directly behind it, the passenger depot is almost center. Today, almost nothing pictured is still there; this area is now the Front Street Shipyard. (Postcard, collection of Matthew D. Cosgro)

Chapter 2

As the country closed in on World War II, the economic pulse of the country quickened and the Belfast and Moosehead Lake was no exception. With gas rationing and the demand for agricultural products rising, the Belfast and Moosehead Lake found itself doing quite well through 1945.

Uncannily similar to the photo from the previous chapter, soldiers have gathered to ride a train off to war in Belfast. This WWII era photo is most likely from 1937 or 1938. Although less than 20 years have passed, the railroad looks quite different then than it did – for one thing, it is now operated as the Belfast and Moosehead Lake, not the Maine Central's Belfast Branch. (McKenna collection, Penobscot Marine Museum)

Like many other communities throughout the United States, the towns along the railroad would send their young boys off to war. Gathered in Belfast, the Belfast and Moosehead Lake carried them from Belfast to Burnham where they would be sent on Maine Central trains to wherever they were destined to go. The railroad also hauled back the coffins of many a hearty young man. Through it all the railroad hauled the freight, carried the passengers and paid its bills.

# Chapter 3

## New Diesels and Profitability – 1946-1959

This unusual view of Burnham Junction was taken on May 31, 1946. You can clearly see the wye, with the Belfast and Moosehead Lake extending into the top right corner. The railroad running left-right is the Maine Central, along with some interchange tracks for freight and the passenger depot that was shared between the two railroads. The two-lane road running left-right is the present-day Route 11/Route 100. Photo taken from Piper Cub 92162, by Al Hurd with Arthur Davis piloting. (Courtesy of the Feero collection)

## Chapter 3

This 1946 view of the roundhouse in Belfast shows a building that looks a bit ratty – it would soon be razed and a two-stall building would replace it.

Just coming through the Beavertail Curve, locomotive 19's days are numbered – July 1946 is the date on this photograph, and by the end of the year, the new GE Diesels will have taken over this railroad. In modern times, this was the site of the short-lived Upper Bridge Station and is now a walking trail. (Photographer unknown, Feero collection.)

The steam locomotive is part of the romantic culture of railroading throughout the world. If you ask an ordinary person to describe a train, quite often a description of a steam locomotive comes out. A roaring fire

– steam whistles piercing the air – a steam locomotive feels like a living beast with a heart and a personality all its own. The reality is that this romantic part of railroading is horribly inefficient and expensive to maintain, but not necessarily expensive to run. As fuel costs ebb and flow, coal is sometimes cheaper than diesel fuel, but what killed the steam locomotive is the expensive and time-consuming repairs and maintenance required to keep a locomotive going. As the World War II wartime material restrictions were finally lifted, the directors of the Belfast and Moosehead Lake went shopping. Although today it is hard to remember, in 1945 diesel electric locomotives were still very rare, particularly on short line railroads that generally operated with second-hand equipment. Late in 1945 the board of directors authorized a representative of the railroad to contact General Electric about a model of diesel electric locomotive that was just entering production. The proposal must have been convincing, as an order was placed early in 1946 and in November of 1946, Locomotives #50 and #51 arrived on home rails. The 600 horsepower, 70-ton diesel electric locomotives were brand new, the first new rolling stock the railroad ever had.

Still in its as-delivered paint scheme, note the small number on the nose of the locomotive next to the headlight, #50 is in Burnham with a passenger train. (Unknown photographer, author's collection.)

# Chapter 3

This Belfast and Moosehead Lake Railroad mixed train is headed east, just over two miles from Belfast on the City Point Trestle. In the background the City Point Station is visible. Other sources state that the station was torn down in 1952. The Belfast and Moosehead Lake received locomotive #51 in November 1946, making this photo between late 1946 and 1952. (Collection of the Penobscot Marine Museum)

The General Electric 70-ton locomotive is an interesting model. Approximately 30 tons lighter than the American Locomotive Company (ALCO) S-1, a competing locomotive with similar horsepower, most major railroads passed on the 70-tonner as being too light for mainline service. Marketed to short lines, industrial railroads and businesses that owned their own railroad track, the 70-ton GE was ideal for a railroad that was replacing tired steam locomotives. #50 and #51 immediately went into service, hauling passengers and freight between Belfast and Burnham. Ever frugal, the railroad management ordered them without the ability to be operated in MU – Multiple Unit – meaning each locomotive required its own crew. In the 1940s, labor was cheap and locomotives were expensive. Overnight, the railroad went from breaking even, to making money. An April 1948 public timetable proudly proclaims 'All Trains Diesel Powered' – the cleaner, less smokey alternative to steam, diesel was a selling point for travelers. Impressed with the GE 70-ton locomotive, the railroad would never buy a different model of diesel locomotive. Still frugal, management increased payments on the first two locomotives and was able to pay them off early.

Being a frugal railroad, the management increased payments on diesel locomotives 50 and 51 and the $104,000 note was ceremonially burned on a pyre of old railroad ties next to the hand-powered Armstrong turntable in June 1950, almost directly under the nose of the steam locomotive that they replaced. (Courtesy of Penobscot Marine Museum)

Chapter 3

A ceremony was held in June of 1950 where the note on the two locomotives was burned in Belfast yard. Steam locomotive #19 was scrapped by the end of June 1950, and the Belfast and Moosehead Lake became fully dieselized.

This photo is undated, but is most likely 1950, the scrapping of Belfast and Moosehead Lake Railroad #19, formerly Bangor and Aroostook Railroad #54 in Belfast Yard.
This photo appeared in the October 1963 issue of *Down East Magazine*, without a detailed caption. (Collection of the Penobscot Marine Museum)

Odd for a shortline used to buying only used equipment, the Belfast and Moosehead Lake would be the second fully dieselized railroad in the state. The Aroostook Valley Railroad was the first to dieselize five years earlier in 1945. May 23, 1951, saw the first run of another brand new 70-ton GE, #52. Although no one knew it at the time, #52 would be the last locomotive the Belfast and Moosehead Lake ever bought new.

#52 was the last locomotive the Belfast and Moosehead Lake would buy new, and in this shot, she is about two months out of the factory. Built in May of 1951, this shot on July 24, 1951, shows 52 weighing cars with the help of the ancient car scale in Belfast Yard. (Photographer unknown, Feero Collection)

Carloads of feed to support the local poultry industry increased dramatically after World War II. In 1946, 714 carloads of feed were handled, up from 421 in 1936.

The original City Point Station was just across the City Point Trestle from Milepost 2. According to this photo, it was torn down in 1952. (Photographer unknown, Feero collection)

Chapter 3

This July 15, 1952, shot of Belfast was taken underneath the passenger station roof. The local Mobil dealer is bringing fuel oil over to the engine house. Speaking of the engine house, this is the all-new one constructed to house the 70-ton GE diesels. Today, very little of this scene remains. (Photographer unknown, Feero collection)

However, in 1953, feed got an additional boost – Brooks Reduction set up shop at Forbes Siding, a couple of miles west of Brooks Station. Brooks Reduction had developed and patented a process to create high-protein chicken feed from byproducts of the poultry processing industry. Later renamed Maine Reduction, then Maine Resources Corporation, Brooks Reduction's successors would last into the 1980s.

On September 27, 1953, John Endler, Jr. spent some time photographing the Belfast and Moosehead Lake. This shot shows locomotive #51 having left part of its mixed train on the main line, using the siding at Brooks Station to deliver cars to the canning plant on the other side of the Route 7 crossing. (Courtesy of the Anthracite Railroads Historical Society.)

By 1956, 3,352 carloads of feed were handled by the railroad, almost an 800 percent increase in 20 years. Commercial poultry production began to boom in Waldo County – with two large processing plants in Belfast and chickens raised throughout Waldo County. Fertilizer and other bulk farming commodities were brought in, processed chickens and the new feed were sent out. Meanwhile, passengers continued to be a source of revenue, although this traffic had steadily declined since the end of World War II.

## Chapter 3

Although largely forgotten today, mail and express were good businesses for most railroads. The Rail Post Office/Baggage car could be the money-producing car on a passenger train. Here we see RPO/Baggage #73 being loaded at Belfast on September 6, 1955. (Photo by and courtesy of Jim Shaughnessy)

The HP Hood Creamery in Unity was still shipping by rail in 1953 and in this photo, captured by John Endler Jr., on September 27, 1953, locomotive #51 had just pulled a milk car from the creamery. (Courtesy of the Anthracite Railroads Historical Society)

It is worth noting that although many shortline railroads are built primarily to serve a single large customer at their end, the Belfast and Moosehead Lake was not. Although the city of Belfast was and is the population center of Waldo County, a Belfast and Moosehead Lake freight train made multiple stops in both directions to switch cars at the various small customers all along the line. In many ways, the Belfast and Moosehead Lake Railroad was Waldo County's freight hauler. Hauling everything from fuel oil to scraps of leather, lumber to chicken feed and vast quantities of pulpwood, this was a true community-serving railroad. Although the schedule would vary over the years, passenger trains would make the round trip from Belfast to Burnham and return. In later years this would be combined with freight, creating a mixed train.

Locomotive #51 has dropped its train on the main, and is heading down the siding next to Unity Station. This station is one of two remaining on the line. (September 27, 1953, photo by John Endler Jr., courtesy of the Anthracite Railroads Historical Society)

At Burnham Junction the Belfast and Moosehead Lake would connect with a Maine Central passenger train and you couldn't ask for a more dramatic contrast – a modern streamlined diesel locomotive with stainless steel passenger cars on one side of the platform and on the other a 70-ton diesel, hauling two steam-era passenger cars. The Belfast and Moosehead Lake must have looked rather small next to the mighty Maine Central, but a more reliable and faithful servant to the people of Waldo County would be hard to find.

# Chapter 3

Burnham Junction was home to a great contrast this day, with the Maine Central switching the interchange with locomotives that each were twice as powerful as the lone 70-tonner on the Belfast and Moosehead Lake side. It would be another nine months before the Maine Central retired steam locomotive #470, while the Belfast and Moosehead Lake had been dieselized for years when this picture was taken. (September 27, 1953, photo by John Endler Jr., courtesy of the Anthracite Railroads Historical Society)

While the Belfast and Moosehead Lake was still hauling Waldo County's products, things were changing. The creameries that once dotted the line were closed one by one as larger, more factory-like creameries were established in centralized locations. Both unprocessed milk and the processed products began to travel longer distances and increasingly this hauling was done by truck.

## The Belfast and Moosehead Lake Railroad

Five months to the day before passenger service ended, #50 and train pose next to the Burnham Junction Station, halfway through the Belfast to Burnham to Belfast train. A mixed train by this time, a hopper car is directly behind 50, with the steam-era RPO baggage and coach bringing up the rear. (October 10, 1959, photo by Clark Frazier, Feero collection.)

# Chapter 4

## End of Passenger Service, Rise of Poultry and the Excursion Business – 1960-1989

Brooks, Maine, specifically the freight house that used to stand next to the passenger station is the location for this shot. Belfast and Moosehead Lake conductor Clyde Page is loading, by hand, packages into a boxcar. This practice became less and less common as packages were increasingly moved by truck. However, into the 1960s the LCL – Less than Carload – freight business was still good. This is most likely early afternoon and the locomotive appears to have cut off the train, leaving it by the passenger station, in order to deliver and pick up cars from businesses in Brooks. The date is unknown, but based upon other photos in the same batch, this is presumed to be no later than March of 1960. (Collection of the Penobscot Marine Museum)

From 1838 when Congress mandated that all railroads would carry US Mail until the 1950s, it could be assumed that your letter or package traveled on at least one railroad during its journey. It was not until first class mail was moved to air transportation and the Interstate Highway System made trucking mail a practical alternative, that the US Postal Service went away from the railroads. The RPO - or Rail Post Office - not only carried the mail but the letters and packages were often sorted by mail employees enroute. Generally attached to passenger trains, owing to higher speeds and tighter schedules, mail was a huge subsidy to often marginal passenger trains, keeping some lines and some entire railroads in the passenger business for years after the ticket sales wouldn't support them. February 5, 1960, saw the last mail run on the Belfast and Moosehead Lake.

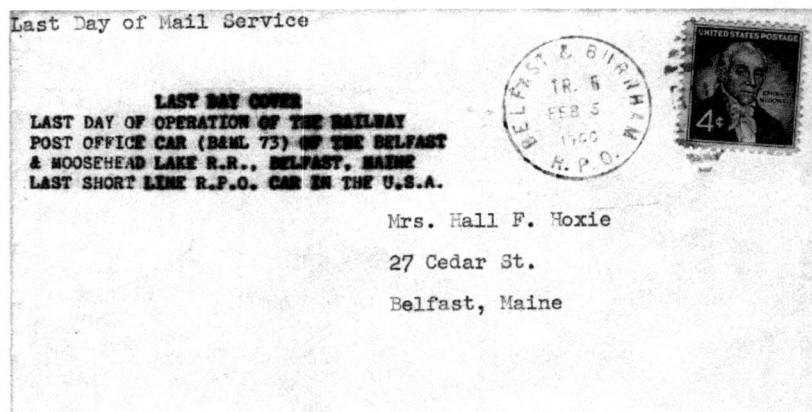

February 5, 1960, marked the last day of Rail Post Office service on the Belfast and Moosehead Lake Railroad. This envelope is in the collection of Belfast Historical Society and Museum.

Railroads in New England are snow fighters. This 1921 Russell snowplow has the duty this day – headed east through Thorndike. (Photo by Tim Franz, January 12, 1984.)

## Chapter 4

Snowplows clear the top of the rail, but the flangeways, where the flanges of each set of wheels ride, are usually cleared by hand. Dwight A. Smith photographed the crew working away at the ice and snow with pick axes and shovels in this February 1971 view. (Courtesy of the Feero collection)

Passenger service could not support itself without the mail contract and despite the railroad's wish to keep passenger service alive, March 10, 1960, saw the last run of regular passenger service on the Belfast and Moosehead Lake Railroad. True to its secondhand equipment image, the passenger cars used were already antiques.

# The Belfast and Moosehead Lake Railroad

Belfast and Moosehead Lake coach #11 is stopped at Thorndike in this photograph. Conductor Pat Shaw is speaking with Station Agent Gertrude Higgins. Known affectionately as "Mrs. Agent," Gertrude Higgins was one of a very small number of female railroad employees in the state and the only female station agent on the Belfast and Moosehead Lake. The date is unknown, but, based upon the lack of a Rail Post Office car, this may be between February and March 1960, the discontinuance of the rail post office car route and the end of passenger service. (Collection of the Penobscot Marine Museum)

Chapter 4

Brooks, Maine, was frequently the spot where trains met and dispatch orders were issued. Station agent Linwood W. Moody, dressed in black, has just finished giving orders to the engineer on #52 and is headed back toward #50 and the caboose to relay those instructions. #52 is crossing Route 7, headed for Belfast. Note the old-style crossing sign on the right, this had largely disappeared with the more common cross shape by this time in history. (Photo by Tom Nemeth, September 5, 1966, courtesy of the Anthracite Railroads Historical Society)

From March of 1960 through 1986, the railroad was freight only, save for a small number of excursions. Some excursions were put on at the request of various railroad enthusiast groups, others were run by the railroad.

## The Belfast and Moosehead Lake Railroad

Although the Maine Central and Bangor and Aroostook Railroads received more coverage for their involvement in Operation Lifesaver, the Belfast and Moosehead Lake did its part too. Operation Lifesaver promotes railroad crossing safety through educational programs. Borrowed Bangor and Aroostook Observation car #107, the Burnt Hill, was used to run an Operation Lifesaver Extra in October 1978. (Photographer unknown, Feero collection)

This 1961 shot shows some of the hard-working Belfast and Moosehead Lake crew. From left to right they are, Wilfred Hall, Kenneth Gibbs, Frank Holms, Chas Page and Walter Bowen. (Photographer unknown, Feero collection)

# Chapter 4

The Belfast and Moosehead Lake was the primary freight connection to Belfast - "The Broiler Capital of the World" - hauling processed chickens out, chicken feed and fertilizer in.

Headed eastbound, just having left Brooks Station a few minutes before, #50's cab is a bit crowded with no caboose on the train this day in November 1973. (Photographer unknown, Feero collection)

Train crews on the Belfast and Moosehead Lake would split the locomotives apart to facilitate switching moves if necessary, then sometimes not bother to put them back on the head end. With only two cars, #52 certainly doesn't need any help with this train. About a mile and a half outside Belfast yard, on the Beavertail curve, today, this is a walking trail. (Photographer unknown, Feero collection.)

As more and more local and interstate freight went to trucks, the poultry industry became increasingly important to the railroad. With only the three original diesel locomotives on the roster and all of them feeling the pinch of years of service, Belfast and Moosehead Lake management went shopping and found Montpelier and Barre Railroad #21 for sale.

## Chapter 4

Although you could easily mistake this for Vermont, Montpelier and Barre #21 is known to the Belfast and Moosehead Lake railroaders as #53. Purchased in 1970, it went into service before being painted. Shown here on the siding in Brooks, crossing Route 7, on July 28, 1970. It would wear three paint schemes within a decade, being painted in the Belfast and Moosehead Lake green with orange and white lettering, then after a rebuild in 1979, would appear in a tasteful and unique red with white pinstripe scheme that it still wears. (Photographer unknown, Feero collection)

A GE 70-ton locomotive, it was the only one on the roster capable of Multiple Unit operation. Added to the roster as #53 in 1970, it would be another 17 years, 1987, before the Berlin Mills Railway would sell their 70-tonners to the Belfast and Moosehead Lake. Berlin Mills #15 became Belfast and Moosehead Lake #54, but Berlin Mills #16 was purchased as a parts source and would never be painted. She lived out the rest of her days in her Berlin Mills #16 paint.

The town of Knox is home to a unique Belfast and Moosehead Lake scene – the main line crosses two driveways and instead of street running, the line has lawn running. Locomotive #53 is towing the just-arrived Berlin Mills Railway #15. (September 17, 1987, photo by Tim Franz.)

Both #51 and #52 would be out of service by 1987 and neither would run again. Feeling the pinch of increased truck use, and having bought running locomotives, #51 and #52 would languish in Belfast yard being picked for parts. Locomotive #52, the newest locomotive on the roster, including all those purchased used, was different from the rest and incorporated many improvements over the original GE 70-ton design. Many cosmetic differences, but several mechanical and electrical upgrades, made the locomotive's parts less useful to the railroad. As a result, #52 remained relatively intact, while #51 and Berlin Mills #16 were used for parts.

# Chapter 4

The song "The Times They Are a-Changin'" by Bob Dylan hadn't even been recorded when Walter Dickey photographed this in March of 1962 – but the times were most certainly changing. The railroad that replaced ships as the primary freight hauler in Waldo county, hauled in the steel for the bridge that would carry highway traffic high above Belfast. Highway improvements would contribute to the railroad losing freight traffic to trucks. (Collection of the Belfast Historical Society and Museum)

In this July 1976 view of the Belfast Yard, we see the water side of the freight station, which by this time was housing the railroad's offices. The track down the right-hand side of the picture continued for some distance along the waterfront at one time, connecting many small businesses with rail. (Photographer unknown, Feero collection)

A rare angle of the yard in Belfast shows how close the railroad and the water really were – the building in the right background is Stinson's cannery. Perhaps the rarest item in this photograph is the kerosene lantern on the top of the switch stand in the foreground on the left, still guarding switch direction in 1973. (Photo by Robert C. Baker Sr., Feero collection.)

Chapter 4

As the 1970s led into the 1980s, the trend was clear - freight was increasingly hauled by truck. Improvements in highways, enabling faster trucking, combined with economic changes, squeezed shortline railroads around the country, the Belfast and Moosehead Lake was no exception. The railroad that was once a diverse freight hauler began to become a single industry railroad - dependent on the poultry industry of Waldo County.

In an unfortunate incident during the spring of 1977, several cars of a westbound train went off the track and toward the water along the Beavertail curve about 1.5 miles out of Belfast. The rumor at the time was that the entire incident would not have happened if the cars, supposed to be in Thorndike, had been left there rather than been pulled all the way to Belfast by mistake. (David Larrabee photo.)

Most derailments are actually very minor events and are easily corrected. This one was not. The railroad had to call in the services of Hulcher Emergency Railroad Services and their team of workers, cranes, heavy lifting equipment and track experts to get the mess cleaned up. (David Larrabee photo, Spring 1977)

Bruce Page, a fourth-generation railroader, is shown here behind the throttle of Locomotive #53. Bruce would serve as both an engineer and Chief Mechanical Officer for the Belfast and Moosehead Lake. This photo originally appeared in the *Waldo Independent*. (Collection of the Belfast Historical Society and Museum)

# Chapter 4

Located at the foot of Main Street, this was one of two grain mills that was in Belfast. (Unknown photographer, 1982, Belfast Historical Society and Museum collection)

Locomotive #51 is flying white flags indicating an 'Extra' or non-scheduled train while rolling over 25 Mile Stream on October 10, 1980. (Tim Franz photo)

The 1980s saw a downward spiral in poultry production and with it, the railroad's freight traffic.

Headed West with a Caboose Extra, #53 pulls its train over the bridge over the aptly named Underpass Road in Brooks, Maine. Maine Reduction, long time rail customer, is just ahead of the train. (October 1983, photographer unknown, Feero collection.)

## Chapter 4

One by one the poultry producers closed or moved. In 1987, it was announced that the Board of Directors of the Belfast and Moosehead Lake elected to operate excursion trains, trying to tap into the growing numbers of tourists coming to Belfast each summer.

Milepost two is just on the other side of the City Point trestle from #53 in this February 1987 view of a winter excursion train. (Photo by Dave Augsburger, Feero collection)

Former Berlin Mills #15 now has her Belfast and Moosehead Lake #54 number and the lettering removed on the hood. It would remain in this paint scheme until painted in the mid-90s. Two ex-Amtrak stainless steel coaches came to the railroad and were used on excursion trains until the Swedish equipment arrived in the early 90s. This Excursion train is headed West over Upper Wescott Stream in this Tim Franz photo on May 14, 1987.

After 27 years, passengers could once again board a train in Belfast. Passengers were carried on everything from dedicated passenger trains, to a coach or caboose on the end of the regular freight train. Initially, these passenger trains consisted of a pair of ex-Amtrak coaches along with some former Maine Central maintenance-of-way equipment that had been retrofitted for passengers. As the popularity grew, two Southern Railroad heavyweight passenger coaches were purchased to accommodate the number of passengers now lining up to ride the rails out of Belfast.

Chapter 4

With the increased commitment to the excursion business, railroad management picked up these two Southern Railway heavyweight passenger cars. Tim Franz photographed both of them in this classic Belfast scene. The railroad used them for several months before painting them. (Photo dated May 27, 1988)

Unfortunately, the railroad's problems were far from over. 1988 saw the first and arguably the biggest in a long line of events that would change the railroad forever. Early in the year, Penobscot Poultry, Maine's last poultry processor and one of the larger employers in Belfast, closed. Before the end of the 1980s, the successor company to Brooks Reduction also closed, ending the outbound feed shipments that had so helped the railroad since 1953. Also in 1988, as part of a bid to keep the railroad solvent, the City of Belfast bought the most valuable asset the Belfast and Moosehead Lake ever had - the waterfront property in Belfast. A lease was worked out, which essentially meant that the City Council could evict the railroad when it felt that the railroad provided insufficient business to Belfast. 1988 did see a published schedule of passenger trains, although it would seem that the effort was half-hearted. The 1988 schedule shows two trains a day on Tuesdays and Thursdays. Only three Saturdays were designated for passenger operations, over the entire summer. By 1989, someone had hit upon the idea of staging a train robbery for the excursion trains. With that the 'Waldo Station Gang' was born. This slapstick comedy routine added to the enjoyment of the trip and to this day, many people remember only the train robbery and nothing else about their train ride. Unlike so many railroads both larger and smaller - the Belfast and

Moosehead Lake would not fade into history without a fight. Alas, the dominoes of change had already begun to fall.

Locomotive #53 works upgrade towards Oak Hill Road Crossing past where the City Point Museum will be built seven years later. August 6, 1989. (Photo by Willam A. Gleason, author's collection)

# Chapter 5

## The End of Freight and Embracing Excursion Trains – 1990-2007

Typical for early 1990s excursion trains, #54 is waiting to depart Brooks, on the return trip to Belfast. (Photographed August 6, 1991, by Fred Jones. Author's collection.)

Without a doubt, the 17-year period between 1990 and 2007 saw the most rapid and radical changes the Belfast and Moosehead Lake Railroad ever experienced. With the commercial poultry industry gone from Waldo County, the chances of freight returning to the railroad in enough quantity for the railroad's survival were dismal. The railroad's attempt at passenger excursions had seen mixed results - although it proved the concept, no one involved in the railroad had previous experience running a tourist attraction. Like many railroads, the Belfast and Moosehead Lake simply hauled what freight was presented to it and many people who visited Belfast, or those that drove through Belfast, were not aware that the railroad still existed, let alone that they could take a ride on it. Marketing to the general public, not businesses, was foreign to most railroaders, not just on the Belfast and Moosehead Lake. As a result, although the tourist excursions did run and did prove that people would ride the train for this purpose, the railroad was by no means thriving.

#54 is about to stop at Waldo Station – perhaps with the Waldo Station Gang robbing the train. (Photo by Ken Houghton, June 11, 1991. Author's collection.)

At the same time, Belfast was reinventing itself as a tourist destination, after decades of being the "Broiler Capital of the World." Poultry may have been a profitable industry for the people of Waldo County, but it had the unfortunate consequence of making many people's first and last impression of Belfast as being one of intolerable smells, causing people to keep going to other destinations on US Route 1. The City of Belfast, being the majority stockholder, decided it was time to sell out. In 1991 the railroad was sold to private investors, headed by Rod Rodrigue. Mr. Rodrigue's previous experience was in the amusement park business and it was felt that he could turn the railroad from a business-friendly freight hauler into a people-friendly attraction. Tourist trains from Belfast to Brooks, a bit over 12 miles from Belfast, operated on a regular schedule. Later, this was cut back to excursions from Belfast to Waldo, 7 miles from the Belfast waterfront.

The station at Brooks became largely unused after excursions were cut back to Waldo. But in 1992 a rather unusual group of visitors descended on the town. The production team from the movie Skylark,

## Chapter 5

the second movie in the Hallmark Hall of Fame Sarah Plain and Tall series, features scenes with actors Glenn Close (playing Sarah) and Christopher Walken (playing Jacob) disembarking from a train onto a station platform. Through movie magic, these scenes were filmed at the Brooks station, using one of the railroad's coaches. Although the station signs proudly proclaim Camden, the station is most certainly Brooks. It is worth noting that there has never been a railroad connection directly to Camden - to get there one would either go via rail to Rockland or Belfast and take some other form of transportation to get to Camden. Why Camden was selected as the rail terminus for the movie is unknown.

Most tourist or historical railroads have at some point in their history a benefactor or friend of the railroad that is in some way responsible for the existence or continuation of the railroad. Bert Clifford was this friend to the Belfast and Moosehead Lake Railroad. A native of Unity, Mr. Clifford made good on his business investments over the years and moved back to Unity a wealthy man. Through his Unity Foundation, he began many civic-minded projects, while running the railroad as a for-profit business. A hook - an attraction - was needed and it was decided that would be a steam locomotive.

Purchased in 1994, locomotive #1149, its tender and a variety of cars were shipped from Sweden into Searsport, Maine. Shown here on the crane, #1149 will shortly be lowered onto American rails for the first time. Operated as a special move, the Bangor and Aroostook railroad would haul the entire train to Northern Maine Junction where the former Maine Central would take over for the trip to Burnham Junction. (June 22, 1994, appearing in the June 23, 1994 *Waldo Independent*, McKenna photo, collection of the Penobscot Marine Museum)

Finding none available across the US that were to his liking, Mr. Clifford bought a 1913 Swedish steam locomotive from the Swedish State Railways. It arrived by ship along with spare parts and many passenger coaches, including dining, sleeping, first and second class coaches. Purchased in 1994, it became the largest operating steam locomotive in Maine and it quickly became quite the attraction. #1149 was named the Spirit of Unity. Saturday July 23, 1994, was a glorious day for the Belfast and Moosehead Lake Railroad. On her first official appearance on the Belfast and Moosehead Lake Railroad, #1149 was brought down to Belfast and fired up, shown for all to see, and it became the first steam locomotive in over 40 years to be turned on Belfast's hand-powered Armstrong turntable. Shortly after the #1149's unveiling, complaints of soot and cinders from the nearby Belfast Boatyard caused Rod Rodrigue to state publicly that "We will not bring the steam engine to Belfast on a regular basis, only a rare occasion." #1149's final appearance in Belfast was on September 24, 1994. Belfast's loss quickly turned into Unity's gain - a new two-stall engine house was constructed, a turntable located and installed, a new station with office space was built next to the existing Unity station and a passenger platform was constructed. #1149 quickly became the public face of the Belfast and Moosehead Lake Railroad and promotional literature from the time reflects that. Unity, never a terribly huge tourist destination, began to become one as word of the steam locomotive spread. Belfast, in the process of promoting its image as a nice, clean, tourist-friendly destination cannot really be blamed for not wanting a coal-fired locomotive in its midst, particularly with the memory of its industrial past so recent. According to newspaper clippings in local papers, as late as 1994 the management of the railroad was still trying to convince the Belfast City Council to allow the railroad to build and service a dock to transload freight from water to rail. This planning and permitting process happened to be going on at the same time as the railroad was fighting a public relations battle over the soot from the steam locomotive. This ship-to-rail facility never got out of the planning stages.

## Chapter 5

While trying to pitch the City of Belfast on the proposed changes to the railroad and the rail-accessible dock, Rod Rodrigue was photographed for the *Waldo Independent*. (Collection of the Belfast Historical Society and Museum)

Locomotive #54 was the most often seen locomotive in the 90s. Here it is eastbound just passing where Winnecook Station was. (Photographer unknown, dated 1995, author's collection.)

In 1995, the right of way containing the railroad's track was sold from the Belfast city line all the way to Burnham Junction. The State of Maine stepped in to preserve the rail corridor and the Belfast and Moosehead Lake became the operator of the track it had previously owned. With steam operations located in Unity and diesel-powered trains running out of Belfast, the Belfast and Moosehead Lake was a very solid seasonal operation. Freight traffic even made a re-appearance, as hopper cars of plastic pellets used in the rope making process re-appeared on the railroad, the first freight after a four-year absence. In Belfast the railroad launched a successful venture called Rail and Sail - you could buy a combined package of a train ride and a cruise on the Riverboat Voyageur. Although it took over 120 years, the railroad's original promoters were finally vindicated as the rail to ship traffic in Belfast became a reality. Each trip featured the Waldo Station Gang robbing the train and a narrated history of the railroad. With boxed lunches offered, it was easy to see why the claim of being "Maine's Best Family Entertainment Value" might well be true.

This mid-1990s view of the Belfast yard shows the Southern Railway coaches being used as a gift shop, coach #15 and former Maine Central equipment used as the telephone museum. All of these would be short-lived uses as the rail was torn up to make more parking room on the waterfront. (Photo from the collection of the Belfast Historical Society and Museum.)

## Chapter 5

The City Point Central became a rail customer in 1996 with this addition of a switch to the Belfast and Moosehead Lake mainline, just towards Belfast off Oak Hill Road. This switch and the tracks it connected would influence modern Belfast and Moosehead Lake Railroad history, more than anyone could imagine at the time. (*Waldo Independent* photograph, Belfast Historical Society and Museum collection.)

The year 1996 saw a small addition to the railroad, but one with long term consequences. Malcolm "Mack" Page received permission to install a switch on the Belfast and Moosehead Lake's main line. Just east of Oak Hill Road in Belfast, this switch and the two tracks it would connect to the main line turned Mr. Page's property into a private car storage facility. Aimed at those with rail cars they wished to leave on active rail, private car owners were willing to pay for the privilege of keeping their cars on Mr. Page's property. Christened the City Point Central, named after the nearby City Point station that once was the first station west of Belfast, Mr. Page's addition of the station from the town of Corinna, Maine, and numerous other artifacts cast off by the Maine Central and Belfast and Moosehead Lake made his collection the first official museum on the Belfast and Moosehead Lake Railroad. No one knew at the time how significant to the railroad this site would become.

## The Belfast and Moosehead Lake Railroad

Mack Page hauled a variety of railroad equipment and structures from various sources to his private museum. Today, this is the eastern terminus of the railroad. (Circa 1999, McKenna photo, *Waldo Independent* collection, Belfast Historical Society and Museum)

The Belfast Chamber of Commerce gave the Belfast and Moosehead Lake Railroad an award in 1996, given by Jim Lovejoy to Bert Clifford and Rod Rodrigue. (Mailloux photo for the *Waldo Independent*, Belfast Historical Society and Museum collection)

Chapter 5

In 1997, the Rodrigue era came to an end. The details of how and why this came about were never made public, but upon leaving Mr. Rodrigue essentially wished the railroad luck in its future endeavors. He also sold his 33 percent share of the company.

When Bert Clifford passed on in 2001, the Belfast and Moosehead Lake's future again became uncertain.

Lacking a proper coal tower, this ramp and loader affair was used to put coal in the tender of #1149 during its time running out of Unity on the Belfast and Moosehead Lake. Somewhat lacking in the appearance department, this arrangement worked very well. (Photo by Shawn Duren, August 4, 2001.)

Locomotive #1149 might have been built in Sweden, but with an American-style whistle on top of her cab, she certainly sounded the part. For many, she was their first, and in some cases only, exposure to a steam locomotive and a better ambassador for steam would be hard to find. Headed west with an excursion train, #1149 will soon be turning on the wye in Burnham to return to Unity. (Photo by Shawn Duren, August 4, 2001.)

Over the next two years things got progressively worse as the Unity Foundation was unwilling to continue to pay for a railroad they didn't want. Railroads are traditionally a high overhead, capital-intensive business, that are highly regulated and difficult to run. Although freight traffic had dwindled to only a handful of cars per year, as late as 2002, freight cars were still on the property. The last freight hauled by the Belfast and Moosehead Lake Railroad were inbound loaded hopper cars of plastic pellets that were transloaded into trucks and taken to Crowe Rope. Crowe was reorganized in 2002, becoming Orion Ropeworks. Orion may have continued to haul plastic pellets by rail, but by 2003, freight was gone.

## Chapter 5

Freight traffic on the Belfast and Moosehead Lake lasted a lot longer than most people were aware. This photo taken on September 1, 2002, shows a hopper car in Unity yard. This is the last photo known to the author showing freight traffic on the Belfast and Moosehead Lake. (Photo by Shawn Duren)

In what would be the final annual City Point Central chartered caboose train, #54 and private cars roll past the closed Stinson canning facility on the Belfast waterfront. The railroad would not run another revenue train out of Belfast yard. (Photo by Shawn Duren, October 24, 2004)

Fortunately, in 2003 the Railstar Corporation entered into a lease-to-buy agreement for the Belfast and Moosehead Lake. Bringing much needed capital investment and an increased budget for track maintenance, things were looking up for the railroad. Paul Hallett was recruited to be the Operations Manager and overall, things improved. One of the clauses of that lease-to-buy agreement was that Railstar needed to maintain the lease with the City of Belfast on the waterfront rail yard and property the railroad had occupied since construction started. One year later, in 2004, Railstar failed to make those rent payments to the City of Belfast. On February 8, 2005, Operations Manager Paul Hallett addressed the Belfast City Council, pleading for mercy. He explained that as part of the growing pains of starting a new business, the bills for rent on the city-owned waterfront property were being sent to the Railstar Corporation owner's personal address. The registered letter sent by the City as required to notify Railstar Corporation that they were behind on rent was signed for by the elderly and unwell mother of the owner and was never seen by the owner. Mr. Hallett held up a box of ticket stubs and quoted figures as to ticket sales for the previous year and spoke of the plans that had yet to be implemented to market the railroad more aggressively in the years to come. Although the City Council voted to give the Railstar Corporation a new one-year lease, Unity Property Management executed the clause in the purchase agreement, citing that the original lease with the City had been broken. Unity Property Management then took the assets of the railroad back and operated one train to clear out the yard in Belfast. On June 9, 2005, Locomotive #54, under the control of veteran Belfast and Moosehead Lake employee Bruce Page, pulled out of Belfast yard for the last time. The train consisted of an odd mix of Belfast and Moosehead Lake history. Locomotive #54 was the last addition to the active locomotive roster and arguably the best locomotive on the railroad. Behind it was a faded red 57-foot mechanical refrigerator car that had been used as a ticket office and gift shop in Belfast. Behind that were a pair of 70-ton locomotives, Berlin Mills #16 and locomotive #52. Pausing to stop at the property line where the City of Belfast-owned land ended, #52 was left behind as a property line marker.

## Chapter 5

When the last train out of Belfast yard departed, locomotive #52 was left at the property line between the railroad and the city of Belfast. (August 2, 2005. Photo by David Larrabee)

The train then proceeded onward to Unity, where it would remain. There were no other operations on the railroad that year. It seemed to most that the railroad was dead. Many said that it was not a viable operation without being able to run out of Belfast. Little time was wasted, and soon the turntable pit was filled in, the rails were removed and gradually, the railroad's mark upon the Belfast waterfront was no more. Given that operations out of Belfast were no longer practical, the right of way from the land owned by the City of Belfast up to the US Route 1 bridge in Belfast was sold to the owner of the nearby food processing plant, effectively ending the railroad's chances of ever returning to the Belfast waterfront. Locomotive #52 was moved under the US Route 1 bridge at the end of the new property line.

When a section of the railroad right-of-way was sold to the adjacent food processing facility, the hulk of locomotive #52 was moved a few hundred feet, under the US Route 1 bridge in Belfast, marking the new end of the property line. Photographed on June 2, 2007, #52 would be reduced to scrap metal within a year. Vandalized, forgotten, abandoned, #52 has the dubious distinction of being the first and, so far, only locomotive to start and end its career on the Belfast and Moosehead Lake Railroad. (Photo by the author)

Chapter 5

Locomotive #1149 pauses at the Burnham Junction wye switch. Fireman Thor Swenson has just thrown it and is directing the locomotive to back up to the train. The train will soon depart for Unity. (October 14, 2006, photo by the author.)

In 2006 the newly created Belfast and Moosehead Lake Railroad Preservation Society took the railroad's assets and began operations as a non-profit. Steam trains operated out of Unity for the year of 2006 and on the face of it, things looked good. Sometime after Bert

Clifford's death, someone decided that the Swedish locomotive could be made to look more American. A large brass number plate was affixed to the front, many of the red pinstripes were removed or painted over and the 'Spirit of Unity' signs disappeared. By 2006, the large number plate had disappeared but the red striping and Spirit of Unity signs never returned. Late in the 2006 season, #1149 was found to be in need of boiler work, that the Belfast and Moosehead Lake Railroad Preservation Society elected not to perform. Alas, the expensive maintenance that caused railroads to retire steam locomotives after World War II still remains.

Conductor Bob Bennett was a summertime fixture on the Belfast and Moosehead Lake, a career school teacher, Mr. Bennett would work for the railroad during the summer school break. Although no one knew it at the time, this would be his last season on the railroad. Shown here taking a picture with a child wearing an engineer's hat. Nurturing children came natural to Mr. Bennett. (July 28, 2007, photo by David Larrabee)

# Chapter 5

The trains that ran during the 2007 season were exclusively hauled by diesel power. August 25, 2007, saw Thor Swenson training as engineer in locomotive #54. Headed east across 25 Mile Stream the train is a little over halfway through its trip from Unity to Burnham and return. (Photo by the author)

Berlin Mills Railway 16 never did have the dignity of being assigned a Belfast and Moosehead Lake number. Shown here on December 5, 2007, by July 1 of 2008, only a pile of parts would remain. (Photo by the author)

The 2007 season operated with only diesel locomotives.

A museum track with the Steam locomotive and other artifacts was constructed, including Berlin Mills #16. Although there were more things to see and do around the train ride, ticket sales did not meet projections as it seemed that the steam locomotive was more of a draw than anyone knew. By the end of the 2007 season, the railroad was headed for shutdown again.

Passing the old creamery in Unity, this often-photographed spot on the railroad has certainly changed. #50 is returning to Unity with a passenger train full of visitors to the Common Ground Country Fair, September 21, 2007. The Common Ground Fair shuttle trains would be the only revenue trains to operate east of Unity for the year of 2007. (Photo by the author)

# Chapter 5

The 'Holiday Trains' in December 2007 were the last revenue trains run by the Belfast and Moosehead Lake Railroad Preservation Society.

Some of the last trains that the Belfast and Moosehead Lake Railroad Preservation Society ran were Holiday Trains. This photo from December 22, 2007, was photographed by the author with lighting provided by Shawn Duren.

# Chapter 6

## The Brooks Preservation Society – 2008-2017

The only train to operate on the railroad for the entire year of 2008 was this equipment move, to move open air car #25 to Brooks from Unity. (November 2, 2008, photo by the author.)

The year 2008 was a low-point in the history of the Belfast and Moosehead Lake Railroad. The yard in Belfast had been lost and one non-profit had tried and failed to operate the line. In March of 2008 locomotive #52, being used as a 70-ton property line marker under the Route 1 Bridge in Belfast was towed out from under the bridge and scrapped. #52, having been bought new by the Belfast and Moosehead Lake, has the dubious honor of being the first locomotive to both start and end her career on the Belfast and Moosehead Lake Railroad. She met her fate within sight of the spot where steam locomotive #19 was scrapped 48 years earlier.

Chapter 6

Berlin Mills Railway #16 was scrapped in Unity yard by the Belfast and Moosehead Lake Railroad Preservation Society. Only a few parts remained on 7-1-2008. (Photo by the author)

By July 1, Berlin Mills #16 was also cut up. Although the Belfast and Moosehead Lake Railroad Preservation Society was the designated operator, no scheduled trains ran on the railroad for the entire year of 2008. Equipment was sold off - with several pieces ending up at the fledgling Downeast Scenic in Ellsworth, Maine. 2008 also saw the rails crossing Route 11/100 on the Bangor leg of the Burnham Junction wye removed and the crossing paved over. Outward appearances were bleak and many thought that the railroad would cease to exist shortly.

Locomotive #50 is pulling what would become the standard excursion consist for trains from 2009 onward--coach #3248 and open air coach #25. These three pieces of equipment would put on many miles together, but this is the first time they all operated together. (Photo by Shawn Duren, April 26, 2009.)

Behind the scenes, changes were coming. The Brooks Preservation Society was formed in 2008, with the purpose of purchasing the Brooks station. Of all the passenger stations on the Belfast and Moosehead Lake, only two were in their original locations, Brooks and Unity. The Brooks station hadn't seen regular service since the early 1990s and was the best preserved of the stations remaining. Soon after negotiating to purchase the property, railroad equipment was offered to Brooks Preservation Society.

Chapter 6

Opening weekend for the Belfast and Moosehead Lake under the Brooks Preservation Society. July 4, 2009, #50 pulled the first scheduled train out of Brooks since 1960. (Photo by the author)

Eventually two locomotives, a variety of track equipment and an open-air passenger car made up the initial Brooks Preservation Society equipment roster. Additional coaches from one of the member's private collection added to the roster and in 2009, scheduled passenger trains began to depart from Brooks Station for the first time in decades. Also introduced in 2009, a first in New England railroading, Brooks Preservation Society offered paying customers the chance to ride a Rail Bike. Previously owned only by individuals, these pedal-powered rail vehicles offered a new way to experience the railroad.

By 2010, locomotive 53 was back on the active roster and pulling regular trains between Brooks and Waldo. Headed back to Brooks, 53 is a bit over a mile and a half from Brooks Station. (July 17, 2010, photo by the author)

Chapter 6

As an end of the season celebration for all the volunteers, Brooks Preservation Society ran a special train all the way to end of track on November 21, 2009. Returning to Brooks, #50 and consist head west over the City Point trestle. (Photo by the author)

Proving that Brooks Preservation Society was truly committed to the entire railroad, On November 21, 2009 the first train ran to Belfast since the train that cleared out Belfast yard in 2005.

For the first year of Brooks Preservation Society operations every crossing had to be flagged by hand. The author is pictured providing crossing protection for an eastbound #50 headed from Brooks to Waldo. (Photo by Shawn Duren, August 29, 2009)

After two years of operations out of Brooks, passenger counts were not meeting expectations. A re-thinking of operations was in order. Belfast remains both the population center and tourist destination in Waldo County and operating trains 12 miles from Belfast seemed to be a great enough distance to keep the casual rider from making the trip. A deal was struck with Unity Property Management, who still owned the railroad from the Route 1 Bridge in Belfast to the Belfast city line and operations moved to a location along the Passagassawaukeag River known as Upper Bridge, a bit over a mile from the waterfront property previously occupied by the railroad.

Chapter 6

Upper Bridge Station was literally a platform next to the tracks and a dirt parking lot. Home of Belfast and Moosehead Lake passenger trains for multiple seasons, operations moved just up the tracks to City Point in 2013. (Photo by David Larrabee, July 24, 2012)

Named for the bridge that once connected the shores of the river, Upper Bridge was a city-owned dirt parking lot. Given that the spot was on the easterly end of the Beavertail Curve, it was a scenic location, but a lack of land available for construction of facilities to support a rail operation at the site made continued operations from this location impractical.

Passengers boarded the trains of the Belfast and Moosehead Lake at the Upper Bridge station during the 2011 season. This afforded photographers the opportunity to photograph trains on the City Point Trestle. #53 is headed west toward Waldo. (Photo by Shawn Duren, August 27, 2011.)

In 2013 after two seasons of operations at Upper Bridge, the operation moved again, to City Point. Located about 2.3 miles from the Belfast waterfront and less than a mile from the Upper Bridge location, the City Point Central became the Eastern terminus of the railroad.

## Chapter 6

Long after the last passenger has left, the sun begins to set over City Point Station. (July 24, 2016, photo by the author)

With a station already on site, a visible and locally known location where railroad equipment already was known to reside, the location was in many ways ideal. After leasing the property for a year, Brooks Preservation Society purchased the property and the majority of operations have run from City Point ever since. By this point, the City of Belfast had purchased the right of way containing the track within its city limits. Brooks Preservation Society leases the portion of the track owned by the City of Belfast to connect with the State of Maine owned rail.

Robert "Bob" Gillam made a career out of working the track for various railroads, starting on the Belfast and Moosehead Lake. After retirement, he came back and functioned as the Roadmaster for Brooks Preservation Society, until his passing in 2016. (July 12, 2009, photo by the author.)

Chapter 6

With years of maintenance being a low priority for Belfast and Moosehead Lake operators, the biggest single challenge Brooks Preservation Society has faced is track maintenance. Volunteers started in 2008 and continue to this day. Mike Francoeur, one of the founding members, sights in a grade stake after some crossing maintenance just outside Unity, May 30, 2009. (Photo by the author)

In order to stabilize Brooks station, the building was raised off the stone blocks and a concrete crawlspace was poured underneath the structure. Susan Gayle photographed the station on September 5, 2013.

Ten miles up the track, the Brooks station hasn't been left unattended - it has received countless hours of work. A new concrete foundation, funded by private donors and the Amherst Railway Society was installed in 2013, ensuring that the station will be around for years to come. Repainted into the Maine Central's gray and green two-tone passenger station scheme, and with interior restoration in progress, Brooks station remains the most historically accurate and well-preserved station on the Belfast and Moosehead Lake Railroad. The station was placed on the National Register of Historic Places in August of 2009.

# Chapter 6

Brooks Station has seen a lot of modifications over the years, but Brooks Preservation Society is working to put the station back to its earlier appearance. (September 4, 2016, photo by the author)

Future plans for the Brooks station site include building a reproduction of the Brooks Freight House that will house a modern photo and historic artifact archive to help preserve the Brooks Preservation Society's growing collection. About two miles further west, near the site of the old Brooks Reduction plant, land is being cleared for a new locomotive and car maintenance and storage facility - the first major construction on the line in decades. In 2015 the first addition in over a decade to the track of the Belfast and Moosehead Lake was completed in City Point. Although minor to some, the addition of the crossover between the two tracks will enable locomotives to run around their train at both City Point and Waldo, increasing the ease of operation on crews.

## The Belfast and Moosehead Lake Railroad

Locomotive #1149 arrived on the Belfast and Moosehead Lake on its own wheels. It would leave on this low flatcar. Destined for Discovery Park of America in Union City, Tennessee, it is not operational. Photo taken on May 23, 2013, by Susan Gayle.

It hasn't been all good news on the railroad preservation front. Not all of the assets of the Belfast and Moosehead Lake Railroad Preservation Society were purchased by the Brooks Preservation Society. Most notably, steam locomotive #1149 was sold to out-of-state interests and shipped out on flatcars in 2013. Prior to that, the Southern Railway heavyweight passenger cars that the railroad used to haul so many excursion trains, went back South, also on flatcars.

In 2014 the new property owner of the Unity station, engine house and yard, had the Brooks Preservation Society remove the tracks leading up to the engine house, turntable and one side track on their property. The majority of the rail removed was kept for future use.

While passengers were boarding trains at Upper Bridge, less than two miles from the site of the old passenger station, in 2011 the engine house on the Belfast waterfront was torn down to make room for the boat yard under construction. Four years later, in 2015, the freight house that had occupied the Belfast waterfront since the railroad was completed was torn down. Despite the best efforts of the City of Belfast to find someone to move the building, funding could not be found.

Chapter 6

With the construction of the Rail Trail slated to start at any time, the Belfast and Moosehead Lake arranged to run one last train over the City Point Trestle, on July 12, 2014. A night photo session was arranged and Shawn Duren and Mike Peverett brought their lighting gear to complete the package. Photographers lined the road bridge parallel to the tracks and #50 pulled the last train across the City Point Trestle. (Photo by the author)

In 2014, a rail trail was established along the over 2 miles of the railroad right of way from the Route 1 bridge in Belfast to Oak Hill Road.

Although rail-banked, this effectively made City Point Station the eastern-most point on the railroad. With the rails removed and trail construction an ongoing project, the 33-mile railroad has been reduced to just over 30.

Officially the City of Belfast calls it the Passy Rail Trail and rather than detracting from the railroad, the rail trail has in fact brought new visibility to the museum and railroad at City Point. Next to the station and museum, a parking area for the trail users has been established. People who thought the railroad was gone, or never even knew it existed, now stop and look at the museum from the trail. Some even find themselves arriving just before a train departs and decide to take a ride!

## The Belfast and Moosehead Lake Railroad

On October 10, 2014, rail removal work was in progress as #50 looks on from what has become the new mainline. (Photo by the author.)

The property that the railroad once occupied on the Belfast waterfront is now occupied by a boat yard. This boat yard is a year-round operation, unlike the seasonal railroad that it replaced. We will never know what would have happened had the railroad remained and the marketing campaign Railstar hinted at launching had taken off. Perhaps the railroad would have turned into an economic boom once again.

Brooks Preservation Society is the first non-profit to successfully operate the Belfast and Moosehead Lake Railroad and is on track to be the longest operator of the railroad since 1991.

Despite being reduced in mileage, the Belfast and Moosehead Lake Railroad continues to survive. A dedicated group of volunteers who share a common passion for railroading keep this railroad going and operating under the name it was chartered under - 150 years ago.

# Chapter 6

Lower Wescott Stream is a beautiful, but almost inaccessible spot on the railroad. Taking advantage of extraordinarily low water, the author photographed #50 making a fall foliage run, heading for Waldo. Executive Director Joe Feero is holding down the conductor's seat.

# About the Author

Joseph T. "Joey" Kelley is a railroad historian, photographer and volunteer with the Brooks Preservation Society. He has been involved with the Belfast and Moosehead Lake Railroad on and off since 2004 and was once a paid employee of the Belfast and Moosehead Lake Railroad Preservation Society. His other passions include photography, motorcycles and restoring antique equipment.

www.ingramcontent.com/pod-product-compliance
Lightning Source LLC
LaVergne TN
LVHW020936090426
835512LV00020B/3387